DYING EMBERS

ARTEMUS CANE

*To the heat of the fire
which forged the blade;
From the blade full of ire
respect must also be paid.*

To make the poem of the human conscience, were it only with reference to a single man, were it only in connection with the basest of men, would be to blend all epics into one superior and definitive epic. Conscience is the chaos of chimeras, of lusts, and of temptations; the furnace of dreams; the lair of ideas of which we are ashamed; it is the pandemonium of sophisms; it is the battlefield of the passions.

Penetrate, at certain hours, past the livid face of a human being who is engaged in reflection, and look behind, gaze into that soul, gaze into that obscurity. There, beneath that external silence, battles of giants, like those recorded in Homer, are in progress; skirmishes of dragons and hydras and swarms of phantoms, as in Milton; visionary circles, as in Dante. What a solemn thing is this infinity which every man bears within him, and which he measures with despair against the caprices of his brain and the actions of his life!

Alighieri one day met with a sinister-looking door, before which he hesitated. Here is one before us, upon whose threshold we hesitate. Let us enter, nevertheless.

-Victor Hugo, *Les Misérables**

*As translated by Isabel F. Hapgood ©1887
Urbana, Illinois: Project Gutenberg. Retrieved May 16, 2020,
from www.gutenberg.org/files/135/135-h/135-h.htm

CONTENTS

CONTENTS

PROEM

This book began many years ago. Its roots go back to before my first publishable poem, before I started writing poetry as a way to cope. It started with a dreadful poem I made for my mom.

I must've been no more than 7 or 8 when I wrote it. Unfortunately, I can't ever forget it, embarrassing as it was. Suffice to say, a poem that rhymes *home* with *gnome* is never going to go over well. It took some time for me to ever return to poetry. But about a decade later I started writing poetry on a regular basis.

Only in the last few years have I written anything I feel confident enough to publish. Yet publication has never been the reason I write. I write so that my pain can become something more than it is. I see it as my soul's attempt at alchemy, to transmute pain into something beautiful and meaningful, something with purpose.

I've found myself encouraged by witnessing others successfully publish their own works to the support and praise of the community, and while I recognize I'm no Poe or Byron, I also realize that it is not skill alone that is valued by supporters of the art. Poets have little to lose and much to gain by sharing their works today, and there is little else I can do but take this next step. If nothing else, I hope this book inspires you, as I am inspired by others who have spilled their hearts with a pen.

I would like to thank the talented lyricists who have inspired me over the years: Roy Khan, Tom Shear, Marshall Mathers III, and Robert Brown. Your music speaks, and has helped me when I needed it most.

I would also like to thank my friends who previewed and appreciated this book, and my dear friends Katelyn and Peter for never giving up on me.

Finally, I would like to thank Edwin Hurdle – your courage is contagious.

DISCLAIMER

This book contains personal works inspired partly by real events and the introspection of the author. However, any similarity to actual persons, living or dead, is purely coincidental. Characters contained within this book are either inspired composites, or entirely fictitious. No identification with actual persons living or dead, places, buildings, or products is intended or should be inferred.

ONE

"I don't want to start any blasphemous rumours,
but I think that God's got a sick sense of humour, and
when I die, I expect to find him laughing..."
– Depeche Mode, *Blasphemous Rumours*

THE LOWEST THING

Picture now, the lowliest,
The saddest wretch, the ugliest
The utmost vile, pathetic whelp
We all know him, it cannot be helped

He is a man so in need of help
A desperate heart, a foolish schlep
To see him kneel, to beg and plead,
So hideous is a man in need

Now, not the apathetic bum
Who asks for coin for drink or crumb
Nay! Tis he! Universal fiend!
Unclean, unwanted, and so, demeaned

He has no friend to be found
No one to defend him now

He kneels and crawls, he moans and bawls
We ask ourselves what became of his balls
So piteous he, and with patience swiftly spent,
Humanity, discontent to leave him present
We send him hence
Lest the hardened walls of our hearts be rent

So oftentimes he'll depart without that which he sought
Though sometimes we'll decide to help the poor sod
Just remember, someday you might walk in his shoes
if Fate hands *you* one too many issues

FOGGY ROAD

Look on in despair
At the boy sitting there

A shivering bloke
Huddled up 'neath the oak

He's been there a while
Saving up for a smile

What's not taken 'way
At the end of the day

A blank check he'll clutch
You may say it's not much

But it's all that he is
All that ever was his

He's looking to barter
But it couldn't be harder

With no good to buy
Nor a peddler pass by

WINTER'S BREATH

Everybody cracks a smile
Until they realize
I'm dying here
I shed a tear
So they divert their eyes

No one wants to warm me
I need too much, I guess
Too weak against my demons
Needs too great to suppress

I feel I understand that love
Could be, if only I would find
Someone a bit more understanding
But am I the one who's blind?

When all the world would throw you away
When nothing now seems clear
Am I insane, are they?
Maybe I should disappear

Broken, battered, still kicked down
I walk along the streets of town
I watch them pass, I see them smile
Every step is another mile

I listen to the forest crack
As winter's breath is felt
Will I ever find a love for me?
Will this icy heart not melt?

PAIN IN THE SHADOW

Pain in the shadow
Joy in the night
The silent god
A boisterous devil
Finding warmth in the moonlight

SHADOW AND COLD

Dying in nightshade, my comforting cloak
Ever since that fateful day, sheltered 'neath the oak
I've been trying to lay to rest the shadow and the cold
But that shivering lad never seems to grow old

The devil I know, he never leaves me 'lone
I'll fill his bowl with vengeance, he'll gnaw to the bone
An egg of pain, abandonment, it's always the same
They can see well my suffering, but they can't say my name

The fog permeated the mind of the boy
When Fate found he'd make such a wonderful toy
An ever-eager heart, a never-ending fight
Still sometimes I return to that day in the night

JUDAS

What were you doing when I met the darkness?
Was it something important?
Why didn't you stay with me?
Where were you when my hands were bound?
Where were you?

What was so interesting to you while I struggled in the black?
Was it meaningful to you?
What sight was so enticing that you walked away?
Where were you?

What did you expect to get out of your errand?
Was it so urgent?
Where were you when I ran for my life?
Where were you?

Who was so dear to you that you gave up on me?
Was he so friendly?
Where were you when my legs gave way?
Where were you?

Why did you feel I was not worth it?
Am I so bad?
When I fell so far, darkhounds nipping at my heels
Where were you?

Who helped the darkness consume my light?
Was it too bright?
Where are you as my enemies surround?

Watching.

GROWING DESPAIR

I have sown this seed
A knife to bleed
My sickle to reap
Mousebane to keep

A friend indeed
For when the need
We both shall die
For when I cry,

That is when she'll drink my tears
Her rain, her sun, my pain and fears
Her life depends upon my sorrow
My fate depends upon tomorrow

For if those heavy storms yet yield
Some hidden path in light revealed
My spirit may find nourishment
Let cast aside the monk his hood

Relieve my second of this duty
Let the hangman rest a spell
Allow my wraith eternity
To live again, freed from Hell

GROWING DESPAIR (CONT'D)

In fog, in cold, in shade, behold
This soul still yearns for sunshine bold
This heart yet reaches for someone to hold
While all along I question, "Why?"

Is there some curse I need to break?
A fiendish foe I've yet to shake?
Is it some fault found within me
That only others are allowed to see?

For I have searched my heathen soul
And found that moths have eaten holes
But even they've left, the spiders too
My portrait paints a dire hue

So I'll feed my foe with every pang
Until we both have had enough
Then, at least, a poetic end
Hope can only sustain so long

ALONG THE WAY

Living in the dark, I am the damned
Long have I struggled through the muck,
the thorns, the pits,
all come without forewarning

Along the way, I lost my heart

For too long I have searched for someone to show me the light
of the world, to be my light and to remind me
where I lost my heart

It is there! I catch glimpses
of the light of the world, the light I lost,
the light my eyes strain to see
The light to guide me back to myself, to where I lost
my heart

I often think I've found my light,
only to find it a pale reflection on a shiny token;
the source of the light is forever hidden,
yet forever I search in vain

I found my heart without aid of light - we fools,
in the dark we trod upon it
Those demons danced along the trail,
our hearts crunched beneath their cloven hooves
as we struggled blindly,
and lost our hearts along the way

ALONG THE WAY (CONT'D)

Living in the dark, I am the damned
Long have I struggled through the muck,
the thorns, the pits,
all come without forewarning

Along the way, I lost myself

I continue to search for someone to show me
the light of the world, to be my light and to remind me
what I am

I am there! I catch glimpses
of the life of what would, the life I lust,
the life that I long to live
The life where I am revealed, where I would find
myself

I often think I live that life,
only as it is revealed a mirage, a dream, a loan;
alone I creep along,
still I search in vain

My heart betrayed, it leapt away - the fool,
it sought the light alone
Without knowledge, it was stretched and torn,
the demons toyed with my foolish heart
as it struggled wildly,
and I lost myself along the way

Living in the dark, I am the damned
Long have I struggled through the muck,
the thorns, the pits,
all come without forewarning

Along the way, I lost.

WHILE ALL ALONG I'M QUESTIONING

God,
Imaginary friend
Invisible foe
Shadowy Freud
Possible fraud

God,
When will it end?
Where will I go?
What should I avoid?
How should I start?

God,
why?

REFLECTIONS OF MAN CONDEMNED

Again I sip from the optimistic chalice
The bitter taste of denial on my lips
My simple cup of pessimism
Fortifies me in my prison

Condemned by man aligned
By some unseen common creed
Aren't I the one maligned
Sent away to rot and bleed

The King of Or has conquered she
Who holds the sword and cannot see
With heavy heart, the honest feather
Lifted aloft into the æther

Love is a gift that was never returned
Hope is a lesson that is never learned
Faith is a body never to be burned
Sacrifice, to a god unconcerned

LAMENTATIONS END

My grave was dug, the rains came down
I clawed the walls, feared I would drown
The choking mud, perpetual pain
I prayed to God once again

Crying out for an oblivious death
For I knew I had not much life left
I mourned the morn, the noon, and soon
I thought the night would die too

I traveled the darkness, made a wish
I watched the waves in anguish
Emergency, a siren's song
Longing to see love emerge…

One leap of faith would lead to another
A swipe to the right, corrected as lovers
The balance restored, see what Fate has in store!
Two decades' reward, give or take

The eye of the storm, the eye of Ra
Gaze down into my grave
Dawn comes again with a brilliant flame!
An angel's face from the blue

I shall die in the place that has no name
Not buried alive by the mud and the rain
I return to that void, pay respect to the pain
Two cents for the eyes, may he not rise again

TWO

"Ruin hath taught me thus to ruminate
That Time will come and take my love away.
This thought is as a death which cannot choose
But weep to have that which it fears to lose."
– William Shakespeare (Sonnet 64)

Love Note

Ambrosia cannot taste
Satin cannot feel
as wonderful as this

No aroma of rose
No sirens' song
can bring to mind such bliss

No sight ever dreamed
Nor dream ever lived
will ever, ever compare

To you, my love,
My heart of hearts
You conquer with a kiss

A Nightmare Awake
(Villanelle Format)

Lovely Endymion, we met in a dream
What a wonderful sleep it was for us
But woe is the greater scheme

Though for eternity it did seem
Carving our love in but one tree of the forest
Lovely Endymion, we loved in a dream

We would venture down to the darkened stream
On returning, watch as the creatures adore us
But woe was the greater scheme

In the field we found such heavy cream
Such a rich path was laid before us
Lovely Endymion, our love was a dream

You allowed your fiends to make you scream
Burning. Watch as the creatures contort us
Tragedy is the final scheme

Ashes rise in a sunbeam
Broken soul, I alone could not restore us
Lovely Endymion, we met in a dream
But woe is the greater scheme

RECKLESS ABANDON

With every single breath, you
Determined to be a deaf-mute
My undying love now dead, moot
What have you done?

Become a thoughtless kine, you
Letting the pain of life though
Lost sight of what matters, blinded true
Just for a little fun...

You will take your last breath, alone
Unwanted once your magic's gone
You threw away the man who stayed
He was the only one.

THE PRINCE AFAR

Do you still court that impish tramp
Who branded you with sinner's stamp?
That jealous fiend with silver tongue
Who killed our love that died so young
Have you cast him out, as you cast me down
From heavenly grace, and heavy crown?
My prince, my lord, my heart's desire
Pray tell you've cast such doubts aside!
Return to me, and return my throne
I'll pay my penance, I shall atone
Show me a sign and I'll slay them all!
Watch dragons, beasts, and demons fall!
I'll rend the walls, I'll scale the peaks
I'll brave the fire, I'll swim the seas
I'll seize the Grail, just to hear you speak
Those words I miss, from lips to kiss
With tender passion, such perfect bliss
I wish to hold you, in day as night
No longer beholden to cold moonlight
For dreams cannot compare to you
Nor memory afford a clearer view
Say the word, we'll rendezvous
Return the magic, remember true
Let demons die and angels sing!
Let love take flight on blessed wing!
By your command we shall reunite
Revive the land we set alight
All will be right again, you'll see!
If only you'd come back to me

"WHEN YOU'RE GOING THROUGH HELL…"
(Long Version)

I love you, I love you, I cannot stop loving you, even as
the day grows dim.
Tomorrow will tell what the weather will spell, but today
I yet feel the sun.
Though darkness looms, and the moon is new,
I cannot but think of you.
Yes, fates may spin, and weave and weft, but there is
no gloom that can compare
To the doom that I have faced, in losing you,
my everything.
I've grieved and wept, yet into further depths
I must still go on.
The path that others paved for me, across the primrose acres.
With good intentions, and all that I have lost because.
So much was taken with so much care,
yet now in Hell I cannot cease,
I must keep moving, I can't look back now, for if I do, for sure
I'll lose the one I love.
Such it was for Orpheus, whose Eurydice forever went.
Because his patient faith was spent.
But look behind through fear or angst, and surely
history will claim again,
Another soul assumed lost and damned, but for
the second chance of Heaven's grace

"WHEN YOU'RE GOING THROUGH HELL…" (CONT'D)

So I flee from my despair, in hope of preserving future hope.
A chance for a chance, and if not redemption,
Tabula rasa for debts eschewed. To begin anew,
never again to be seen in such a ruddy hue.

As I stride across these
dying embers, I cannot but
remember you.
Yet all the same I must outpace
the demons haunting this place.

Though incubus may ride by moon,
And revelations blind by noon,
Through fog of doubt, and lightning's shock
I will survive this journey through the dark

Pursuit

Over the river
Through the wood
A bullet of silver
I did what I could

It wasn't enough
Now I've lost my friend
All you see as the wolf
Is me cloaked in red

I ignored the danger
We didn't seek help
Then came the change
And you lost yourself

I cannot stop running
Because if I do
I'll be eaten alive
By the memory of you

Moving On

Like the ghost of a blizzard
From the winter we shared so warm
I look amongst the lost world
You hide up here alone

I wonder if you remember me
Or have you hidden me away
Another ghost beneath the sheet
You hide up here so safe

Snowflakes falling towards the sun
A hidden breeze in a sunbeam
I watch the ashes, the unsettled dust
In your attic, like a dream

WINTER'S BITE – HAIKU #1

Cold irony
rebound more troublesome
than the first shot

ROMANCE OR LOVE

Romance is a flower that will soon enough wilt
Causing young faces precious tears to be spilt
Perhaps they'll pluck another, and so on, until
They find sustenance in a seed less beautiful
So they search through the garden for a peach or a pear
And they find that it only satisfies for part of the year
A little season or two, and they venture to forage
But everything withers, leaving them
discouraged
So they turn to the hunt, loosing their volleys
Hoping to find nourishment with this folly
These lonely hearts may not last through the frost
But they may yet learn to love if they can afford the cost

Inventory

Torn down, shoved aside
Sealed and marked
In a cardboard box, ready for the ride
The moving truck is parked outside

It was never a question of if, but when
So much was built upon a dream
But as I take inventory of all I own
I realize we weren't much of a team even then

It was I who built upon the dream
A dream deferred, but not denied
I've dealt already with the fragile things
And the worthless trinkets I leave behind

WAKE

As I trespass across the garden whence you bloomed so bold
Withering as your spectres flash in the recess of my mind's eye
Haunting for their warmth, disturbing my temperate cold
Closing the shutters, as if it were much more than a sigh

Treading lightly, lest I disturb your slumber
Reading with lights aplenty, such as to ward off something
untoward
Silence breeds fresh fiends, it hurts to remember
My head bleeds back into my empty heart

As I tread the same paths which led to your demise
Paved with chrysanthemums and good intent
What caused you to change so, I can only surmise
Leaving nothing behind 'fore your descent

Fading night and finding naught, I return to my cot
Perhaps it is not for me to find a way into your world
In such a grave image are my moments often shot
Though perhaps tomorrow I may finally move forward

THREE

"He who strives on and lives to strive
Can earn redemption still."
-Angels *Faust: Part Two*

ONCE UPON A CASTLE

There is a king
In a faraway land
With the simple things
He's quite content

He has him a wife
A comfortable queen
She brings him strife
This I have seen

They had a young daughter
and then, a prince
Noble like none other
I haven't seen him since

The prince, well, he died
He died in name
He died in mind
It's all just the same

All's left is the girl
A weedy tavern wench
Rebels 'gainst the real
Her thirst can't be quenched

She's 'come quite the steed
So I hear. Indeed,
at night she's a mare
Just in that, she succeeds

The king keeps ahold
His kin spends his gold
This kingdom, so fragile
It was home, for a while

TREACHERY

West of the gate
Another tower gone
Taken by our foe
Sealed is our fate

Bubbling up the 'well
Trampling the lawn
We've nowhere left to go
Our bastion of Hell

The walls are crushing arms
The sky is crying flame
But the earth begins to thunder
Waves crash into the farms

Our allies come to fight
By God, we'll do the same!
'Til now I dared not wonder
We might yet survive this night!

REBELLION

We live our war, though you'll never see
Fighting for our right to live, and little more
Life isn't fair, isn't it true...
I certainly have less than you
We struggle and try to break free, to fly
Or at least to save ourselves from drowning
For if we deny *ourselves* opportunity,
How would we ever find the strength to smile?

The weights we bear, they tug and tear
Dragging us ever lower...
The depths await our weakened spirits.
Shall we willingly go there?
I say no.
We'll fight until even Heaven can hear it!

'Til the bitter end, we deny you all
The satisfaction of seeing us fall
For what else is there to *do but* try?
We fight because there's hope,
We fight because we must,
We fight for the *chance* to fly.

SEASON'S END
PART ONE – SPENSERIAN SONNET #1

Just so, a new moon has risen high
And my sun has set in scarlet veils
'Twas to see, such a sorry sight
But a starry night doth yet prevails

The creaky captain hoists the sails
The lamed wolf now hunts alone
For man and beast the chilling gales
Have cut their way down to the bone

Yes, winter's eve has set the tone
For each, a darker path begun
The silent tower, a looming gravestone
A violent, overpowering beacon

This night, as waves bombard the rocks
I rise to see what stranger knocks…

LEAVES

I still remember, sometime before,
When I was green as new spring,
I was connected

But one day, I was floating,
At the mercy of the wind
I was disconnected

As the wind carried me away,
Powerless to control where I'd go
I began to decay

Sometimes I would rest,
I thought I'd found a home,
But then the wind would come again

Today, even the wind has left me
I'm too heavy for it to carry me further

A Pebble

A pebble.
Grains of sand flow
around me. I am too heavy
to join in their swimming.
They are too busy to stay
for long.

WINTER MOURNING
TETRACTYS PRACTICE #1

Rise.
So low.
Like snowmen,
they call me friend,
but watch them fade in the warmth of my glow...

My First
Successful Poem:

At the end of all
there is a fall
when man must turn to dust
and all of our technology
will melt and turn to rust
we sit and cry
with dying eyes
long gone without seeing
not knowing how we fell this far
us mighty human beings

To Market

Charcoal shades drift across an emerald ocean
Electric potential summons me from the depths
Feline Memory a torrential encore in my mind
Recalls the hunt of a wolf, alone in the night

Quixotic endeavors summoning chaotic cleavers
No thunder to warn of the tower's demise
Jupiter's house rains lightning on the reluctant victor
As Boreas steals away his defiant cries

Letters now sent to the powerful variator
Looking on into the eyeless soul of Earth
Save my heart once more before I take flight anew
Pursuing sustenance I may not find today

I AWAIT YOUR RESPONSE
COMPASS POEM
(ORIGINAL FORMAT)

keys pressed
combination
to my heart   a reaching
out of time   out of sync
I will send, then
patience

RESOLUTION

And so die the embers
The ashes resting undisturbed
On a cold night in December
In an untended hearth

Not a crack, not a flickering
The passion has dissipated
On a solemn New Year's Evening
The fireworks have faded

PHOENIX

That old hound, shut behind my door
A deep breath of autumn dew
Burning decay blossoms before my eyes
As the fog begins to fade

Caribbean sea washes away the starry void
A family of ten play in the dunes
Waves crash, roaring past my home
This world now exposed, I take another step…

ABOUT THE AUTHOR

Artemus Cane has been writing poetry and stories for friends and family for many years. A lover of music and fiction, you'll often find him locked away at night in his Michigan home consumed by a good book or his favorite songs.

He prefers writing poetry over reading it, cats over people, Pandora over Spotify, Netflix over Hulu, spilled milk over crying, eggs over medium, and really overdoing things.

He is not a vampire.